Preface

In today's world instead of asking why do we need sales? We can rephrase it by saying, what will happen if sales don't happen! The truth is that sales are inevitable in business and everyone needs it.

Strategies of sales are different, yet the purpose remains the same. This book will take you through the dimensions of sales viewed from different angles. Becoming a sales expert is very easy when the understanding of small things become predominant over old stereotype thinking. It comes embedded in our DNA, from generation to generation sales exist in our system and from the time we are born we realize it's potential. This book assures you the thorough understanding and possibilities of sales.

There are multiple variables which are always linked to the core of sales. Even sales has got culture and after reading through this book you can get a feel of it. People can copy sales strategies, but they can never copy the sales culture. This book will be the perfect tool you can utilize to overcome all the negative stereotype thinking's related to sales. Nowadays we can see that many trainer positions have been created in the corporate to enhance and harness the true potential of sales person. This book will also make us understand that sales is growing, to be precise we can say that sales is getting mature. This book teaches you that sales are not our opponent but should be our partner. We have read many books, attended many presentations but have we ever thought why we still fail, it's not because they did not teach us viable points but it's because we have not improvised. The tour of this book will make you a better professional and teach you to be a sales alchemist. After reading through this book, your motto should be to improvise with every step or move you make. Sales do not limit us to any theories or books but is an open ocean and has got infinite ways in which it can be viewed. Knowing sales is a necessity in business as oxygen is for breathing. This book features all the necessary ingredients which are really necessary for understanding and enjoying the beauty of sales. This book will be kept short and easy for sales people to understand sales process in an easy manner.

About the author

The author of the book is Mr. MITHUN DEVADAS who has been a sales enthusiast for many years and currently giving consulting in African and Middle East countries for different clienteles. He started of his career as a runner in a restaurant whose primary job was to clean tables as well as invite prospects standing outside the restaurant in South Africa's beautiful province Durban. He knew the importance of his job role, he used to attract the prospect by speaking loud "Fresh chips, fresh sea food ".He was a skinny Indian who had gone for his higher secondary education in South Africa and had learnt that advertising the restaurant in a funny voice did make a great impact. That was the beginning of his career and later brought fancy imitation ornaments and cosmetics realizing the potential of the South African market. He was doing door to door sales and started experiencing sales in the real world at the age of 16.

He later started working in different sales and marketing domains in Middle East as well in India. His greatest ambition was to become the greatest sales person ever and he was working as a free lance trainer selling his knowledge and experience to companies. Later on he was hired by a well known Suzuki car dealership in India, as a sales trainer.

He is a post graduate in masters of business administration with dual specialization in marketing and human resource. This is his first book through which he wants to share his experience and knowledge. He wanted to write a book for all sales people around the world, which was simple but really powerful.

CONTENT

1. Introduction
2. Lead and prospect
3. Technology and social media
4. Law of averages
5. Grooming, Hygiene and Self marketing Tool
6. Product knowledge
7. Body language
8. Handling Gate keeper and taking an appointment
9. Handling objections
10. Closing techniques
11. Referrals
12. Follow up
13. Sales presentation
14. Motivational quotes

1. Introduction

Let us get into the world of sales; everyone has different views about sales. Some people say sales is the most difficult thing in this world, some say sales is a job which is not for the faint hearted. But have you seen or heard sales people who are minting money or enjoying a lavish life. First of all we have to remove all the negative thoughts about sales which come into our mind. We might have come across thousands of definitions of sales but in this book let us look into a practical definition.

"Sales is the ultimate result of marketing, aimed at convincing individuals or group of individuals to our desired thought"

Some people think that sales happen only when we join an organization but the fact is that sales happen from the time we are born.

1. How did we convince our parents for excursion or bike or smart phone?
2. How did we convince our parents for sweets?
3. How did we convince our girl friend to fall in love with us?
4. How did we clear the interview?

Sales happen in different scenarios of life, we are the product and when our necessity is fulfilled sales happen. Sales happen everywhere in relationship, business, government etc… but why do we fail to witness it? It's because we find it hard to see beyond our stereotype thoughts. When we see many sales people resigning in insurance, banking, automobile industry, why do we fail to see the people making millions in these same companies. Those people who don't leave the organizations are not magicians but the true sales warriors who have understood how things work. If a barber is made to do a carpenters work he will surely fail but with some exception. But imagine if the same barber has undergone carpentry training, he will surely excel with some practice. Same is to be understood in the area of salespeople who excel have understood the concept of sales through experience or understood it through training or under strong leadership. In the coming topics we will be discussing about all the important aspects to hit home run in sales. Definitely sales is not based on luck or tantric mantras but purely based on our understanding of small things and improvisation. How does a hawker or vegetable seller easily sell his products, he has not gone to any university or attended any training programs but sells successfully after learning sales techniques passed on to him from previous generation .They really do excel in what they do and earn their livelihood. Sales do not exist in isolation, but is dependent on different variables.

In the coming chapters we will be discussing about different variables as well as different approaches we can make in sales to make it more effective. Long time back competition was less and possibilities of sales was more but nowadays people have become more intelligent and the necessity to take a different path has becomes very important.

Sales is purely based on the conviction we have on our product, until unless we are not convinced with our product we will never be able to sell the product. The more convinced you are about your product, easier it becomes for you to sell the product. It gets reflected in your body language and tone of your voice. Sales are moreover like selling your enthusiasm to your prospect, you have to pass on your enthusiasm to your prospect and it will do the magic for sure. Coming chapters in this book will make you understand the art of sales. In Sales what we have to understand is that until unless we convince ourselves that we love and trust the product we won't be able to sell the product to others. There is no other job in this world like sales which is full of fun and freedom, you have the liberty to decide how much money you want to make. You don't need to sit in your desk the whole day getting bored doing the same task again and again. Sales makes you meet different people from different cultures,society,race,age,designation,geographical area etc and you get to learn a lot and make solid contacts. If you want to become a successful business man in future then the best job to do is sales. You get to learn about the psychology of buyers while you are doing sales, which become very much important for business success. The ultimate aim will be to bring "Moment of truth" in sales. When you exceed satisfaction in an efficient manner, you lead to moment of truth. A customer who has attained moment of truth will definitely and surely give referrals to sales person .As a sales person we should make customer for lifetime and build a relation so strong that we can rely on the customer anytime we want .For example: You sold a car to a doctor when you were working for an automobile company and later when you joined as a medical representative you sold the same doctor medicines. When you make customer for lifetime, your referral pipeline will never dry up and as a sales person you will be successful all the time.

2. Leads and Prospect

In sales leads and prospect play an important role, but many have misunderstood the real meaning of both. Lead can be prospect but not necessarily all leads can be prospect. When we advertise in the market and if any one calls us then it becomes an enquiry. When this enquiry becomes more promising, then we call it as lead. A qualified lead is called as prospect and the process involving all this called as prospecting. Prospecting is very much important in sales as we are utilizing company's resources and time.

When we conduct a marketing campaign many people call and make a visit, thus giving us many leads. Other way to get good leads is by visiting as many people as we can, this directly improves the chance for us to get more prospects. Nowadays it has been found that sales people do not only rely on company advertising strategies rather they run their own campaign. They utilize social media marketing as the best tool to advertise about them and their product. A professional sales person will utilize each and every chance he gets; sales people should make sure that they talk to as many people as they can. There were cases when a sales person got good leads and prospects while talking to co passengers in train, plane, bus etc…..A sales person will never miss out any opportunity he gets with people.

Social media

1. LinkedIn :(Utilize professional network-post, share etc)
2. Face book :(Post pictures, description or face book advertisement)
3. WhatsApp :(Broadcast different people with latest offer schemes etc)
4. YouTube: (A YouTube video with the product presentation and sales persons mobile number) etc.

The reason why many sales person fail is because they take things for granted. An accountant's job is to do accounting job from morning to evening but he/she cannot move out of the company as they are having desk job. In case of sales people they have the liberty to go out and work. There is no other job in this world which has so much freedom, but sales people misuse this freedom and this is the reason why many sales people fail. Once they are out of office they waste their quality time and most of them utilize this time to do their personal things. Sales people should make sure that they make maximum calls or make maximum visits to get maximum leads. Life of a sales person is such that while travelling he meets different people and through them they get many leads which becomes their future prospect. Example: An automobile sales person drinking coffee in a restaurant will drop his business card at the owner's desk or manager's desk while leaving, in order to promote vehicle sales. In short sales people should make sure to utilize all broadcasting and non broadcasting channels.

Leads pipeline sources

1. E marketing and social media campaigns
2. Exhibition and Tradeshows
3. Networking
4. Direct mailing or sms services
5. Referral system
6. Word of mouth marketing
7. Telemarketing
8. Direct sales and marketing
9. Yellow pages
10. Private database provider companies
11. Internet-Blogs (sign in), webinar, newsletter
12. Social media –YouTube, twitter, face book etc.

A sales pipeline is the way through which sales people get their leads and prospects. An intelligent sales person will make sure that he does not have single sales pipeline but has got multiple pipelines. This way he/she

can ensure that they don't run out of prospect or leads throughout the year. Nowadays sales people have new strategy and they have started socializing as much as they can. Meeting the right type of lead or prospect is also very important, as it saves more time and resources. For example you can join premium gym and while working out you can socialize with other people. Here people will be more relaxed, but never start sales process until unless you get to know them very well.

They should also not feel that you are stalking them or invading their privacy. Other places you can socialize and get leads are

1. Jogging time
2. Grocery shop
3. Birthday party
4. Marriage function
5. Charity events
6. Clubs and association

While targeting leads and prospect make sure that you hit the right audience example: effective selling of sports bikes can happen between the age group 18-35(Go to college area), cruiser bikes can be sold to age group 35-65(Go to club area).Always make sure that you thank the people who give details of leads and prospect, try to give them small gifts .Which in return will get you more leads and prospects. Even enquiries coming to our office or company can be sorted and converted to good leads or prospects. It will be better if we do a proper research on our prospect before approaching them, researching will help us   prepare for the sales

process. We have to do research about our product and our competitors product .It will tell us about the high and low points of our product and our competitors product .This will help us get prepared in advance for prospects difficult questions and the outcome will be success.

Advantages of researching

1. Confidence
2. Facts presentation
3. More closing etc

Tip: Never write down the details of leads or prospect in a piece of paper or diary but maintain it in excel sheet or some software. Always keep a duplicate copy, in case of loss or damage.

3. Technology and social media ethics

We are glad that we have technology advancements in every possible way we can imagine. Today we can get connected to our prospect using video chat,facebook,watsapp,voice call or even video conferencing etc .The truth is that many of us still fail to utilize it to the full ,when the prospect are not reserved or conservative like before. They do like us to connect with them and provide them maximum information via all this mediums.

In some conservative societies we have to be very careful with ladies or higher officials who are really busy and think that invading their privacy is a crime. In WhatsApp we can broadcast our messages to a particular group of prospect and inform them about latest updates. We can even wish our prospect and make use of social media to circulate marketing materials or other informations.Only thing we have to be careful is that they should not feel that we are stalking them. If the prospect gets offended, we have to make sure that we apologize to them immediately. It will be better to take permission before initiating contact through social media or other aspects .You have to keep in touch with the prospect even if the prospect withdraws from the deal at the last minute example: wishing him good morning, happy Christmas, happy diwali etc.In this manner we can build a positive relationship with the prospect. You have to build good personal relationship through social media with people who have rejected your offer. This way we can get more reference from him and you will definitely succeed next time. Today technology is growing so powerful that connecting with the prospect is getting easier. Prospect are also using latest technology to get more intelligent, henceforth it will be always better to get updated with our own product and our competitors product knowledge. Using social media we can definitely improvise our personal relationship with prospect.

Do's

1. Always wish them using social media

2. Always wish them during festivals and occasions

3. Always forward them the latest schemes offers

4. Always inform them about new product or service launch

5. Always keep them updated about the sales process

6. Always use salutations like Mr., Mrs., Ms, M/S etc

7. Always ask permission before you add them in face book, WhatsApp etc

Don'ts

1. Don't stalk them
2. Don't flirt with female prospect
3. Don't be casual with them
4. Avoid late night chats
5. Keep your messages simple and short
6. Don't overcrowd with more documents or pictures
7. Don't indulge in religious or sensitive talks

We all use smart phones but make sure that we always have a nice and smooth ringtone which don't tamper with the positive thinking of a prospect. Imagine a situation when the prospect is thinking in his mind about buying the product and suddenly your phone rings with loud ringtone, he/she will definitely get deviated. We should always make sure that whatever electronic items like laptop, tab, Smartphone etc we are carrying should be free of dust and damaged cover. Always make sure that our phone should be in silent while we are talking with our prospect. Always make sure that you save document or pictures in Smartphone, so that we can share it with our prospect in a jiffy. Today even in WhatsApp we can share pictures, documents etc.Technology has improved so much that it has made our life so easy and productive. We can get value for money for every second we spend using technology. Always make sure that your electronic gadgets are free of virus and free of unwanted files in the desktop which will again slow down your system and create a negative image. We can use our Smartphone to set reminders, appointments, conference calls etc…We can do so much with the technology that we can save lot of time as well as keep in touch with everyone in and around us. Smart phone is such a powerful tool filled with so many utilities that many of the sales people today completely depend on Smartphone .Usage of a good quality smart phone with longer battery life is prescribed for making life easy for sales people. The only challenge is to keep yourself updated with the technologies and utilize it to the full all the time. It will be really better if sales people are well equipped with knowledge of social media applications and other computer skills to enhance their productivity .It also helps in time management which is very important in sales. Today things have changed and technology plays an important role in executing sales

4. Law of averages

Law of averages is one of the most debated topics in sales, as salespeople do not believe in law of averages but still at the end do follow a pattern of law of averages. Law of averages no more remains a layman's term, but has become more important in sales.

If people run this world and people are billions in number then definitely law of averages exist, in sales if we follow the pattern of law of averages then definitely success is inevitatble.Law of averages tell us that maximum sales closure is directly proportional to meeting maximum prospects or leads. Law of averages says that we should not find a comfort zone in sales and stay behind it, rather we should never stop. Example: If we toss two one dollar coins simultaneously for one minute then the probability of getting more heads or more tails by each person will depend upon the number of tosses each individual has made in one minute. A medical representative will be more successful if he meets more doctors than his allocated target, an automobile dealer's executive will have more chance to sell more cars if he meets more and more people within a short span of time. Law of averages may or may not take into consideration the skills of an executive but rather will depend more upon the desire of consumer/prospect to buy our services or products. Law of averages requires less skill and more hardwork, so a person who is using law of averages will be doing hard work rather than smart work. A person either depends on smart work or hardwork, the question is why he doesn't depend on both.

If a sales person combines hard work with smart work then things will be very easy and the results will be astonishing. Many people see law of averages as just layman's theory and take law of averages as old school sales. But have we forgotten that in today's world we are using law of averages in marketing and sales in many ways. Why do we advertise in broadcasting and non broadcasting channels, it is very simple we are trying to apply law of averages. The more reach we have, better the chances are for us to close a deal. In short what we can say is we have to work beyond our target and have patience.

Example

1. Direct sales people should meet 10 leads instead of 5
2. Tele callers should call 120 prospects instead of 70
3. Corporate sales people should meet more purchase managers than planned etc……….

5. Grooming, Hygiene and Self marketing Tool

Grooming and cleanliness has got a very important role to play in professionalism. Each society has its own way of welcoming it, grooming is essential to portray ones positive energy and attitude. In sales grooming plays a very important role as it also plays the part of trust building. Before we even start talking to a prospect, prospect notices our grooming and cleanliness .Sales is a psychological process, in which one of the variables which decide closing is grooming and cleanliness. When we get involved in a conversation with the prospect, the prospect will be watching our every move.

Grooming along with dressing and hygiene are very important, as 55% of the evaluation done by the prospect is based on these factors. Birds and animals groom themselves by tucking their feathers or smoothing their fur, some animals even take bath like elephants to make them cool and clean. We humans also have a long history where in kings and emperors used to decorate themselves with precious stones and precious linens so as to look more appealing or different. From ancient time people used to make themselves smell good using attar and other materials. To smell good and remain clean was a matter of luxury in those times. Always looking good and elegant was a way to attract opposite sex and also to sell that we are trustworthy. Grooming can be defined as
"The art of presenting oneself in a presentable and acceptable pattern"

Prospect needs tons of confidence and patience during the sales process. They would like to consider us as professional consultants whom they can rely during the time of buying. It is truly said "First impression is the best impression"; in sales we should not fail to make that positive impression. Grooming may vary with culture and different geographical locations, but the ultimate aim is to make our self look acceptable.

It's true that some people even without proper grooming sell services and products easily, as said sales is the combination of many parameters and getting grooming parameter in check will lead to more sales. While we are walking in a busy street we meet different people, but before even talking with any person we make judgment of each and every person we see. If we see a person with blazer we think that he might be a senior person working in a company. Then we see another person with stained clothes, we analyze that this particular person is working in a workshop or farm. The same happens in sales, prospect makes an impression about you the moment he/she sees your dressing and prospect gains or lose confidence based on that.

If the prospect makes a positive impression about you means it adds leverage to your sales process and chances of closing the sales will be more. A good grooming of oneself will lead to the below effects.

- ➢ Professional acceptance
- ➢ Self confidence
- ➢ Confidence of prospect
- ➢ Branding of company
- ➢ More productivity

Cleanliness refers to the way in which we keep our self clean and hygiene. In sales this is very important as we meet and greet lot of people while we are doing sales. Just imagine we are talking to a person and there is a foul smell coming out of his mouth, what will we think about this person? Making a good first impression is very challenging but attainable, if we take care of few things which we will be covering in this session.

Before going for sales make sure that you adhere to this checklist and the results will be fruitful for sure. Dressing and accessories play an important role in making one look different and to make a personal statement. Why do we add accessories to our car or bike, it's to make our car or bike look different and make a personal statement. In the same manner dressing and accessories give us a different look and define us of our personality.

In sales it is very important to make one different from each other as we face tough competition from our competitors. We cannot wear casual shoes with formal clothes and we cannot wear a funky watch with a professional blazer . In this book we will go through checklist, it may vary with different cultures and different company policies. Format of dressing and accessories vary from country to country, hence this book will give some ideas on what to do and what not to do in general.

<u>Hair</u>

- Use only formal hairstyle
- Hair should not fall over eyes
- Don't color your hair
- It should be free from head lice and dandruff
- Don't use too much gel or oil
- Sideburn should be till half of the ear
- Hair fall should be treated

Ears

- Keep your ears clean from wax
- Trim the ear hairs

Nose

- Use handkerchief in case of running nose
- Trim the hair inside nose
- Nose hole should be free from mucus and dust
- Don't dig inside nose hole in front of prospect

Teeth and Tongue

- Teeth should be free from yellow stain
- Wash your teeth after breakfast, lunch and dinner
- Use clove or mouth freshener to keep your mouth odor free
- Don't chew gum or other tobacco product during job
- Use tongue cleaner to clean your tongue
- Brush your teeth two times in a day
- Avoid food stains in your mouth
- If teeth is broken fix it to make it look neat and healthy

Finger nails and toe nails

- Should not use dark nail polish-use body color nail polish
- Trim your finger nails and toe nails
- Don't have dirt inside toe and finger nails
- Don't use multicolor nail polish

Body odor

- Use only mild perfumes
- Don't cause perfume stains in your clothes
- Use deodorant in armpits
- Change clothes with sweat

Eyes

- Avoid eye mucus
- Don't use too much eye liner and eye shading
- Wash your eyes after bike ride
- Avoid meeting prospect with eye infection

Cosmetic

- Avoid too much foundation
- Avoid too much make up
- Use mild make up
- Don't use dark lipstick
- Don't use too much cream
- Don't keep your skin too oily or too dry

Beard and Moustache

- Always trim beard and moustache properly
- Don't color your beard or moustache
- Keep beard and moustache according to the culture of company
- Avoid funky beard and moustache arrangement
- Avoid beard subtle.

Smoking

- Wash your hands after smoking
- Chew a gum or mouth freshener before meeting prospect
- Don't smoke in front of the prospect

Clothes

- Always wear clothes of right fit
- Wear uniform if the company is providing
- Avoid using too dark clothes
- Always iron wrinkled clothes
- Always avoid stained clothes
- Avoid damaged or smelling clothes
- Don't put too many things inside pocket
- Use only formal attire in accordance with the culture of soceity and country
- Avoid using too shiny clothes

Ornaments and Spectacles

- Avoid using too much ornaments
- Don't use too much bright colored frames for spectacles
- Don't use hanging earrings instead use studs
- Use simple ornaments
- Avoid dirty or faded ornaments

Pen

- Should use good quality blue or black pen
- Avoid multicolored pens
- Avoid using pen without cap
- Avoid using pen with damage

Wallet

- Use good quality leather wallet
- Should not be bulky with too much things inside
- Should be of single color

Belt

- Should use good quality leather belt
- Avoid multi color
- Don't use big buckles or fancy buckles
- Avoid using damaged belts
- Belt should be the color of shoes

Ladies hand bag

- Should be of single color
- Should not be bulky with too many things inside
- Should not use damaged handbag
- Use good quality leather handbags
- Should not be stained

Shoes and ladies sandals

- Should use good quality leather or artificial leather shoes
- Should use formal shoes
- Avoid using damaged or stained shoes
- Ladies should not use too much heel
- Ladies should avoid using too fancy sandals
- Shoes should be always polished
- Dark brown ,brown and black colored shoes are preferred
- If using lace make sure you tie it properly

Socks

- Should wear full length socks
- Avoid dirty and smelling socks
- New pair of socks should be used daily
- Damaged socks should be avoided

Business card holder

- Use formal business card holders
- Use single color business card holder
- Steel color and wooden touch preferred

Watch

- Should avoid using multicolor watches
- Should use formal watches
- Steel strap or leather strap preferred
- Avoid bulky watches
- Make sure strap is free of stains

Note: Avoid showing tattooed body parts, as it might create negative impression.

6. Product knowledge

Product knowledge is very important in sales as without it we are just talking; if we need to talk in an intelligent manner we should have good product knowledge. We should have product knowledge of our product as well as through knowledge of our competitor's product.

"An investment in knowledge pays the best interest"
Benjamin Franklin

Product knowledge will help the sales personal overcome objection and also make them answer difficult questions. It helps them to build trust, as a person with good product knowledge is assumed to be more reliable by the prospect. A prospect always wants to buy from sales people who are having thorough knowledge of the product and expects them to make prospect understand about the product. In today's world prospects are very intelligent and we should make sure that we keep our self updated and informed in order to keep up with the market. We should not even underestimate the knowledge of small kids accompanying their parents, in automobile industry small kids tend to know more things than the car sales man. We cannot say it is the ability of small kids rather we can say it is the inability of sales people to keep themselves updated. Today people just can Google up and know about anything through their Smartphone, henceforth it becomes the ultimate requirement of sales people to enhance their product knowledge from time to time.

Sources of product knowledge
1. Marketing literature
2. Trade journals
3. Google
4. Website
5. Trainings
A. On the job training
B. Classroom training
6. Company brochure etc…..

While studying about product, we should make sure that we learn about its benefits and feature. Prospect should understand why the product is distinct from other products and also what they will gain by purchasing the product.

Example: Smart Car A –Feature: VGT turbocharger   Benefit: More performance and power
Smart Car B-Feature: CVT gear box   Benefit: Easy and smooth gear shifting

Prospect always want to make intelligent purchase and product knowledge will make them realize that they are doing the right thing by buying our product. We should make sure that while explaining feature, advantage and benefit never exaggerate or tell lies.

Make sure that you apologize and tell them that you will get back with the information, in case you are unable to answer any product related queries. Presentation of feature, advantage and benefit should be done in a beautiful way as it enhances the chances of sales.

Normal way

"Sir your vehicle comes with ABS"

With beautiful presentation

"Sir your car comes with highly advanced breaking technology called as ABS which gives you and your family safe journey"

What you should know about your product

1. Colour
2. Model and design
3. Manufacturing process
4. Type of materials used
5. Unique selling preposition
6. History
7. Add on in your product etc

Product knowledge helps you to talk like an expert and prospects treats you with respect. There were many cases when the prospect has even made complaint against the sales personal for misleading them with wrong information's .A happy prospect is the one who gets all the information and feels that he is part of a "win win " situation.

7. Body language

In sales body language plays a vital role as prospect makes majority of evaluation in the first 5 seconds of the initial contact. A positive body language helps us to make a very good impression in front of our prospect. Body language can be more precisely defined as an art of non verbal communication. One who has mastered the art of body language has got more edge over others.

Nowadays learning body language has become a necessity in sales and sales people are giving more priority to learn about body language. Some of the body language is learnt with our social experience, just like how our mother knows about our happiness and sadness by just looking at our face. Observation plays a vital role in body language and we should give more importance to the tiny details. In this book we will learn about few body languages, which will prove beneficial for us to make positive decisions. Learning body language not only helps us in sales, but also in our personal life eradicating negative situations. The easiest way to learn body language is by observing people around us, the best place would be a railway station or a social gathering where we can see a mixture of different personalities.

Body language is such a powerful tool that many sales people are attending crash courses in body language. Everybody uses body language interpretation even without learning it.

We all are born with body language skills; even animals use body language to a great extent example: A dog wagging its tail, it's an indication of loyalty or affection. Experience will make us perfect in body language, but at the same time keen observation of minute details also plays a vital role.

When we are having a conversation with prospect make sure that we act according to the body language of the prospect and we have a solution for the negative body language depicted. Body language never is wrong but sometimes our interpretation has to be adjusted according to the situation for example A person having closed arms is an indication of negative attitude, but it can also happen if he/she is in a cold place. Henceforth we should be very careful in the interpretation part, as similar conditions may prevail.

7.1 Evaluation making posture: If you notice a prospect sitting in this position he is definitely making a decision which is not a favorable one. He does not trust you and he is surely planning to say no to you. If the prospect is saying that he will get to you means ,he is never going to get back to you. In this scenario it will be better if we show him facts and figures , as he is not going to believe a word what you are going to say .Once you show him facts and figures with laptop presentation or by showing him any documents he will come to a positive stance.

7.2 Nose rub: When somebody rubs his/her nose while talking, it means that he/she is telling a lie. If they say yes it means no and if they say no it means yes. It can be used by the speaker to hide a lie or can be used by the listener to show that he is listening to a lie.

7.3 Eye rub: Eye rub is a gesture shown by a person who feels that speaker is telling a lie. In order to avoid looking at him he/she will rub his eye gently. So in sales scenario if the prospect rubs his eyes during the conversation it means that he /she does not trust your words.

7.4 Open body language: Open body language sign is when somebody exposes his inner body and also exposes his palm to the opposite person. In this stance they don't cross their arms and their arms are always open. This is when the prospect is making a positive decision and has got a good opinion about us and our product.

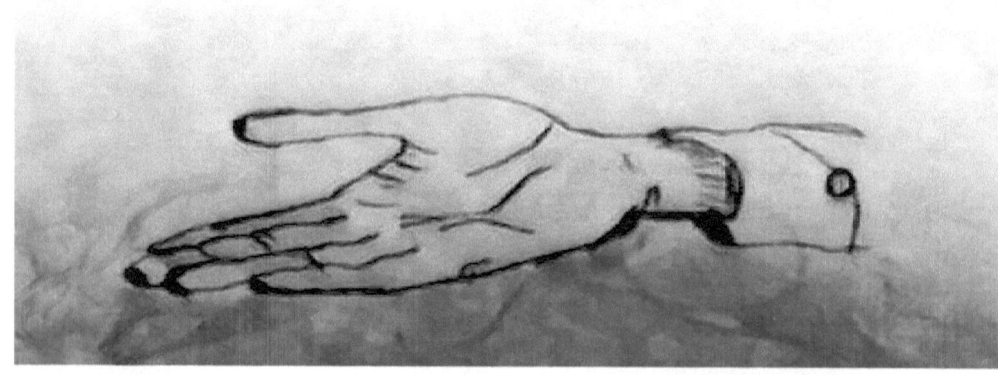

7.5 Submissive palm position: This is a also a good sign while we are doing sales because the prospect or lead is willing to buy product form us and is willing to listen to us. This is part of positive body language and we can think of a positive outcome. In this stance the prospect or lead is having a palm up position.

7.6 Aggressive palm position: In this stance palms are closed almost like a fist and one finger is pointed at an object or person. In this prospect is getting really aggressive and the best way would be to wind up the meeting and keep it for another day or time.

7.7 Dominant palm position: It is the total opposite of submissive palm position and has the palms facing down. When we see the prospect or lead keeping their palm in this manner, it means that they are of dominant nature. This type of people are very difficult to control and we need patience to handle them.

7.8 Handshakes:

7.8.1 Wrong type of handshake: This type of handshake should be avoided at all the cost as it creates wrong impression. Our elbow should bend while we make handshake and we should only reach for handshake from close proximity.

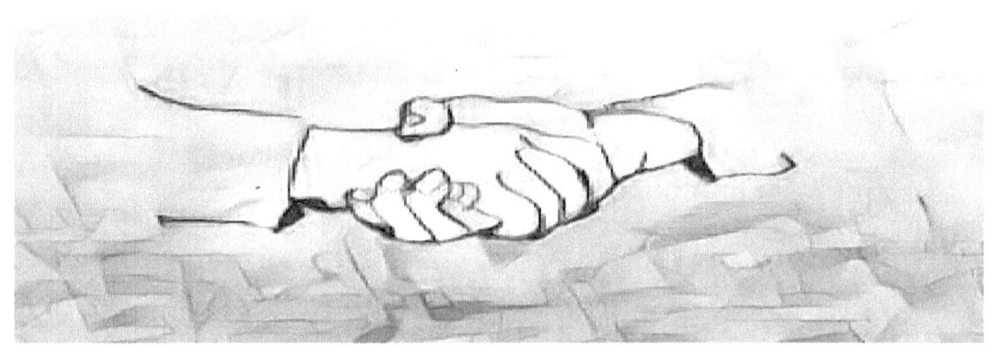

7.8.2 Taking the control: In this handshake the person whose palm is on top is the person who is taking control of the situation and is of dominant nature. So if you are shaking hands with this person and your palm is below means the other person wants to control you.

7.8.3 Bone crushing handshake: Never ever try to do this kind of handshake as it is the most negative form of handshake. This type of handshake crushes other persons palm and makes him/her angry. It is always said that we should give a firm handshake but that does not mean to crush other person's hand.

7.8.4 Dead fish handshake: This type of handshake should also not be given as it gives the person at the other end the feeling that we are having no confidence .It spoils the first impression and at later stage closing will be difficult.

7.8.5 Correct handshake: This type of handshake is always welcomed with a positive smile and should be practiced for a positive outcome in sales. While doing this type of handshake a loose or a too firm handshake should be avoided.

7.8.6 Glove handshake: This type of handshake is mainly given by politicians and sometimes even referred to as politician's handshake. This a fake type of handshake in which the person attempting the glove handshake is going to do the exact opposite of what he has promised.

7.9 Closed body language: It is the exact opposite of the open body language and in this the person will close his arms and sometimes even legs might be crossed. In this scenario the person is totally negative and is difficult to convince, by showing him facts and figures we can make him to open his crossed arms. You can also make the person open his arms by talking in favor of the person or by stop talking what is hurting him/her. We have to be careful while interpreting this body language, as sometimes a person who is feeling cold might also cross his/her arm and it should not be misunderstood for negative attitude.

46

7.10 Hand clenching lower, middle and higher: Hand clenching is sign which means that the person is having a negative thought or negative attitudes .Higher the hand is clenched the higher the person's negative attitude.

7.11 Positive hand rub: This gesture is done by even kids when they feel really happy. The same is done by adults when they feel good about our product and the offer we give. This is a positive sign and you are sure to close the deal with easiness.

7.12 Raised steeple and lowered steeple: This kind of gesture is a positive attitude and also shows the superior nature of the person who is showing the steeple position. Higher steeple means that the person is doing the talking and lowered steeple means the person is listening. We have to give utmost respect to the person with the steeple position as he/she might not take it very well. Most of the time they are managers or people with senior positions who are very confident about themselves.

7.13 Thumps up position: Thumps up position while arms folded is not a positive gesture because it implies superiority, negativity and defensive nature of the person showing it.

7.14 Mouth guard expression/Nose touch/Eye rub: This gesture can be shown by the speaker as well as the listener. It can be used by the speaker to tell a lie and is also used by listener to show disagreement towards speakers lie.

7.15 Ear rub and neck scratch: Ear rub gesture is used by the listener to convey a message of disagreement of speakers lie. Neck scratch is done with the index finger near the neck area and is an indication of doubt and confusion.

7.16 Collar pull: This gesture is shown when the speaker is telling a lie to the listener and is trying to hide his feeling or emotions.

7.17 Males and female version chin stroke: Chin stroke is done by the listener as an indication of negative thought about the speaker .Chin stroke is done with thumb supporting the chin and fingers pointing away. Don't allow this kind of gesture for a prolonged period as it may hinder sales process.

7.18 Arm cross::It is a sign of negative attitude and is way to tell the speaker that he/she is against their decision or action.

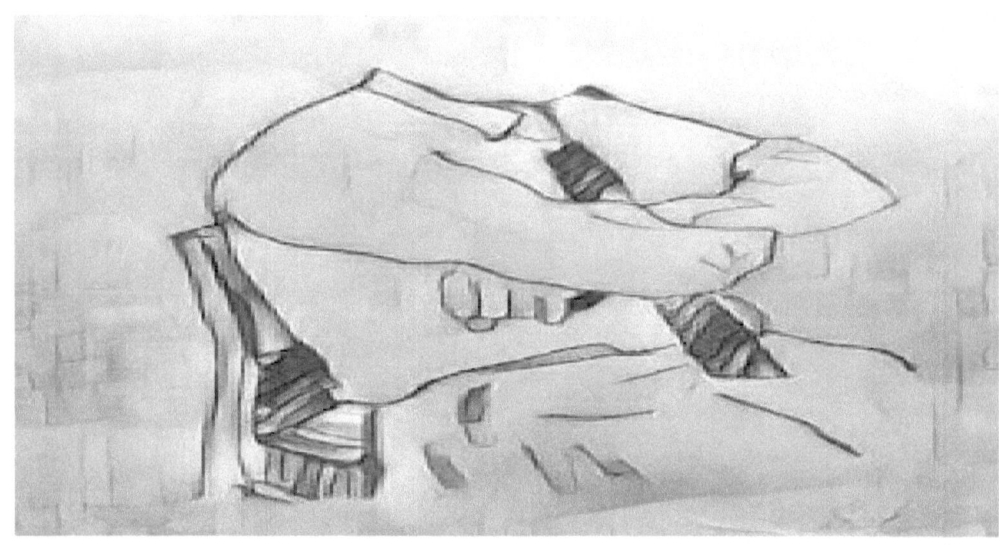

7.19 Arm cross with fist display: It shows that the person we are talking with is really hostile and difficult to control. It will be better to wind up the conversation or even better to change the topic of the conversation to avoid hostility.

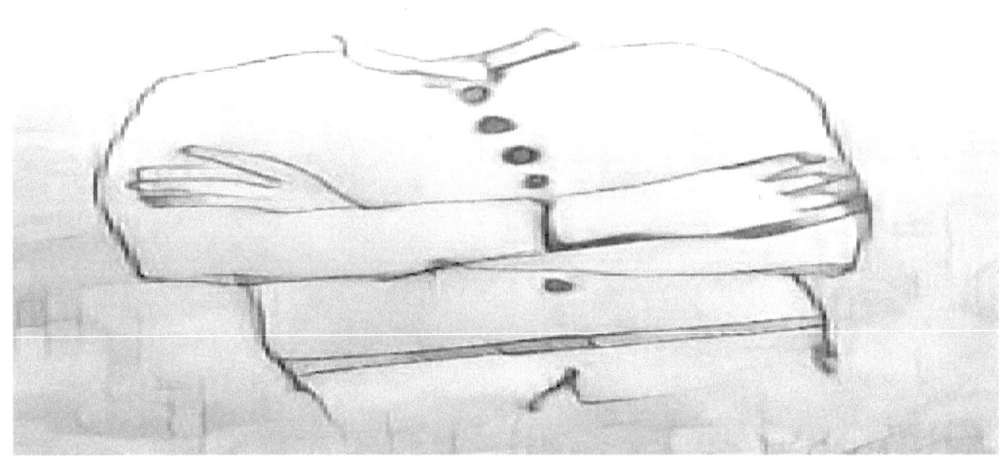

7.20 Firm stand cross: In this posture it implies that the person has already taken a firm decision and is not going to change from it. The only way we can overcome this is by making them talk to our existing happy customer.

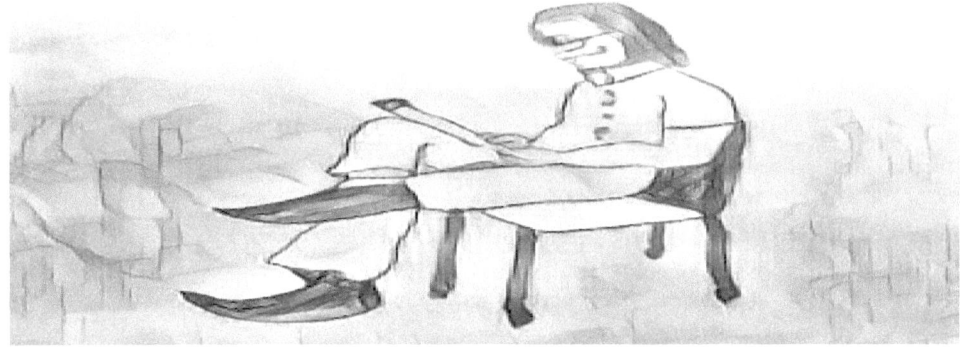

7.21 Superior attitude: This gesture is shown by people who think they are far superior to all others and know all the things in this world. It is really difficult to handle this kind of people until unless we have facts and figures to show them.

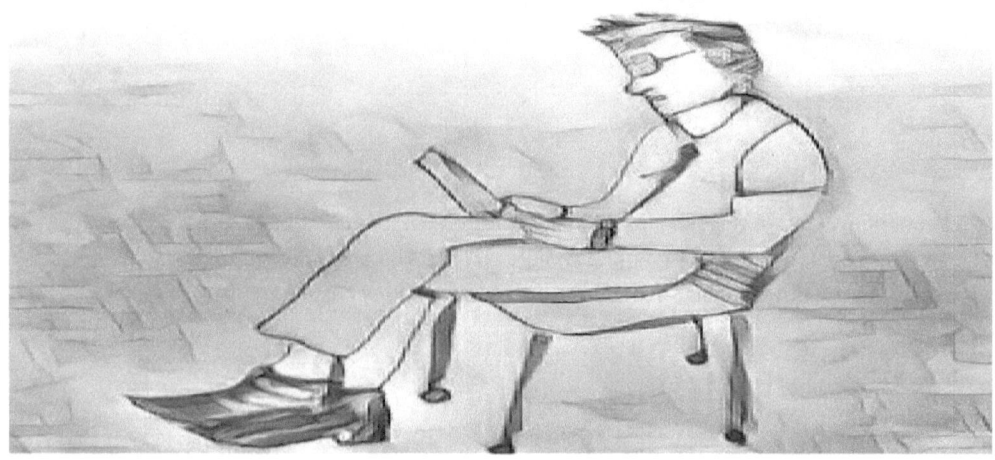

7.22 Normal Leg cross: It is mainly done by the people who are having reserved or defensive attitude and it should be carefully interpreted as sometimes it may be due to uncomfortable seating position.

7.23 Ankle lock: This type of gesture is shown when the person is negative and hostile towards the speaker. Fist is clenched while resting it on the knee or on arm rest of chair.

7.24 Neutral and interested head positions: When the head is not tilted and is in steady position, it means that the person has a neutral stand. It means that the person has not made any decision and has maintained a neutral ground. Prospect is interested in your product and services if he is showing tilted head with exposed neck.

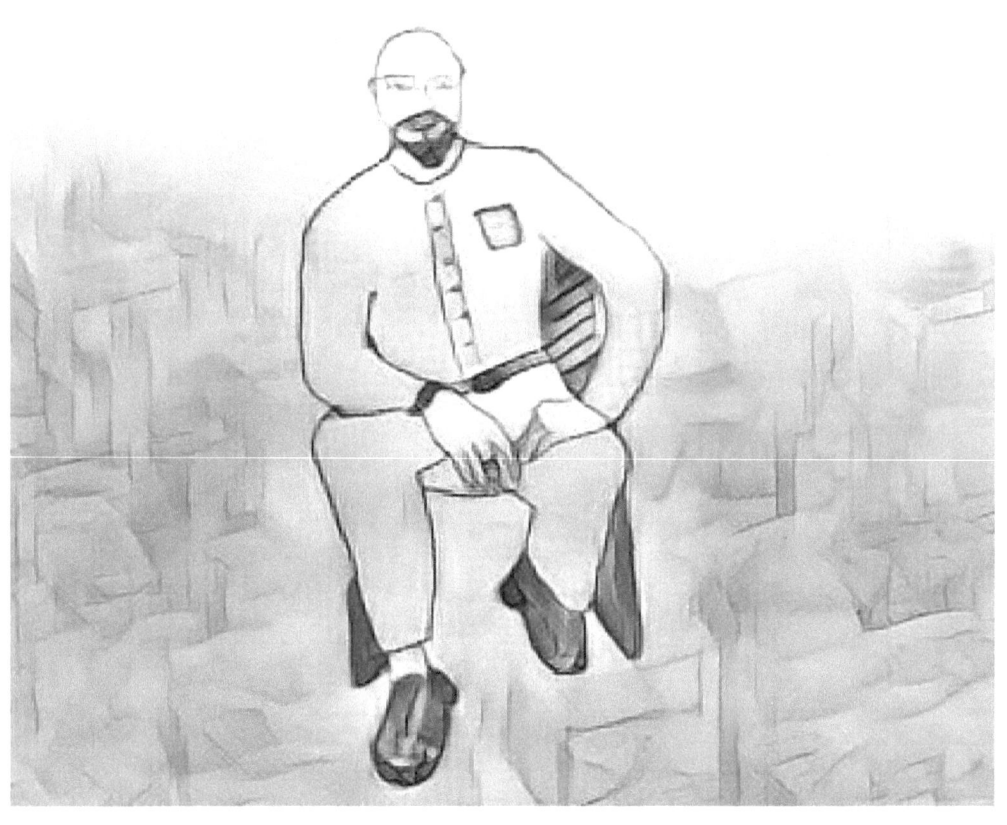

7.25 Ready to Proceed: This gesture means that the prospect is in a hurry or is not having patience .The best way to handle this situation will be to postpone the meeting or to offer the prospect some lucrative offers .Prospect will only be in a comfortable seating position when he/she is hearing something good. If you see the prospect in this posture, then it's time to offer them good offers.

7.26 Making a decision: In this the prospect is thinking about the possibilities and in this scenario one must make sure to remain calm and give time for him/her to think. Prospect will slowly pull his beard or even slightly pull his chin. Here the magic key is silence, let the prospect talk first to break the silence.

8. Handling Gatekeepers and taking appointments

Sales people face lot of challenges in their job and one such challenge is the 'Gatekeeper'. These are the people who become a barrier between sales people and decision maker while making the first cold call. They pose serious challenges nowadays as they are not the same gatekeepers of the past. Nowadays gatekeepers are educated and experienced, they not only handle calls but also have some kind of authority. They can be receptionist, secretary or even any other office staffs. Never take gatekeepers for granted as they can cut you out from the main decision maker. Many sales people learn to handle gatekeepers through their experience but in today's competitive world things have become even more difficult. You might be thinking that you are the only person engaged with the gatekeeper, in reality they might be receiving minimum of 50- 100 calls in a day. Gate keepers can become your biggest friend or even become your biggest barrier, it all depend upon how you view them and how you deal with them. Gatekeepers are called as information pool and we can utilize gatekeepers to learn many things about the decision maker, thus complimenting research.

Advantages of gatekeepers
1. Provide more information about the decision maker
2. Provide name of the decision maker
3. Support in sales

There are basically two types of gatekeeper's submissive gatekeeper and dominant gatekeeper. Submissive gatekeeper are people who give less resistance and try to connect you to the decision maker without asking much questions ,whereas dominant gatekeepers are the ones who create resistance or barrier between the sales people and the decision maker by asking questions. Whenever you talk to a submissive gatekeeper make sure that you ask for the name before the conversation, if the gatekeeper fails to give their name.

"Good morning my name is biju, who am I speaking to"

Throughout the conversation make sure that you use their name. When you use their name it adds personalization and yields good result. You can also note down gatekeepers name in your follow up data sheet, so that next time when you call you call them by their name. Always ask for advice from gatekeepers and give them good respect throughout the conversation. Gatekeepers get happy when you ask advice and will surely treat you different from other sales people.

"Ms Rita what time will be best for me to talk to Mr. Das"

In some companies gatekeepers are given training to cut out sales people calling them. If you don't act different, you will just become like a normal sales person. In case of a dominant gatekeeper these things won't work out as they are already expecting sales people and they decide whether you are the right or wrong person to be connected with the decision maker. In this case you have to do lot of practice before even attempting to make the call. Within the first few seconds you will come to know whether you are dealing with submissive gatekeeper or dominant gatekeeper.

Tone and language of dominant gatekeeper will be harsh and rude, timing is very important .You too have to talk to them in a dominant manner and tell them that you don't have time to waste. When they hear your heavy tone they will get confused thinking you are not the normal sales person they encounter everyday. Before attempting this techniques make sure that you are not rude and have mock practice with your friends. Even wishing them is not necessary here to some extent.

Gatekeeper: "Good morning my name is Sarah, how may I assist you"

Sales person:"Hey Sarah is James there, connect me to him urgently"
This all depends upon your tone and if you do it beautifully then you can straight away talk to the decision maker without any hassles.

Tips to bypass gatekeepers

1. Odd time calling technique: Gatekeepers mostly work according to the strict office timings and this can become a boon for us. Try to call decision makers during luck break, early hours or even during after office hours. This is because when you call them during these hours instead of trained gatekeeper attending the call some other staffs will answer the call making things easy for us.

2. Email technique: Try to get the email of decision maker and draft a mail which highlights the feature, advantage and benefit of the product with heavy discounts keeping timeline. Request for an appointment for further discussion .This way you cut out the gatekeepers from your sales process.

3. Danger technique: Ask the gatekeeper some difficult questions which they are unable to answer and in this manner prevent them from asking you more questions.

"Do you know latest rules of fire and safety act of India, according to it your company is in trouble? I need to urgently speak with your manager". This will be applicable for a sales person who is selling fire and safety equipments.

4. Take away weapon technique: In this techniques we have to use their own weapon against them. They will always say either they are busy or they are not available. Sometimes they straight away say that their company is already using another companies product cutting you out from the decision maker. Prepare a script in which you tell those things in such a way that they are unable to use their own script.

"Dear Sarah I know that they are very busy people and might not be available all time in the office, but I would like to know when I can call them to fix an appointment"

All this depends upon the way you speak fast and the tone of your voice. In this technique make sure that you don't give chance for the gatekeeper to speak.

5. **Secret technique:** Don't try to sell the product to the gatekeeper as it will make gatekeeper cut you out from reaching the decision maker. Gatekeepers might be receiving calls from over hundred callers each day and they know if they don't cut you out their boss will be angry on them. They are trained to only let in important calls and not all calls disturbing the decision makers.

Taking an appointment

Once you pass the gatekeeper, it's time for us to take the appointment. Appointment is more effective than a direct walk in attempt. This can be effective only if it is in alliance with law of averages, as meeting few customers won't yield the result. After appointment is fixed with the decision maker, even the gatekeeper might have blocked the time period or conference room for you.

When you get an appointment the decision maker might have invited other decision makers also to the meeting, thus improving the chances of your sale. Decision maker will be prepared for the appointment and he will even make note of things he would like to discuss in particular with you. After bypassing the gatekeeper and before taking appointment one must make sure that they are well prepared. Some companies have even set call centers to maximize appointment and for getting maximum sales. Appointments are set with decision makers consent and it is more effective than the normal walk in, where sales people have to put lot of effort. While taking a sales appointment be sure to keep your conversation as short as possible. This is because we have to respect and value the time of the decision makers, as they might have attended the call thinking that the gatekeeper has let in the right caller. Always ask for the time and date of appointment before ending the conversation with the decision maker, so that the decision maker along with you can plan.

Technique for taking an appointment

1. Take away weapon technique: You can use the same technique used earlier on the gatekeeper. This technique helps the sales people to make the decision maker not use their script on you.

2. Super purpose and offer technique: When you are talking with the decision maker, always tell them about the benefits of the product and the special discount or offer they are going to get by dealing with them.

3. Question mark technique: If you ask a question, they surely will have to answer you. This is a psychological move and it really works out. This all depends on again the tone of your voice in which you are talking to them. A slight fluctuation in your tone will be understood by the decision maker and chances of an appointment will be minimal.

Sales person: "Good morning sir my name is Rahall from VBN company, I am sorry I called you during busy hours of the day and I will make sure that I wind up my conversation within 3 minutes"

Decision maker: "Yes, go on"

Sales person: "sir since you are lion's club member, we are planning to give you our product for 15% discount and for 2 years you are eligible for free service. Sir for further discussion on this, kindly request for an appointment. Will it be okay if I meet you on Tuesday 10 am?"

Decision maker: "Hmm...Tuesday I have meeting with my junior managers, can you make it on Wednesday"
Sales person: "Sir what time should I meet you on Wednesday?"
Decision maker: "11 am will be fine, thank you "

9. HANDLING OBJECTIONS

In this world people fear about sales because of the objections raised by the prospect, they will definitely have objections as today's prospects have become more smart and intelligent. Objections can be raised at any point of the sales process and it becomes the duty of sales person to overcome it with a smile. Sales person cannot run away from objection and it becomes an integral part of sales. We do sales in our daily life and also handle objections in our day to day life. When your father said no to a sports bike, how did you convince him for buying the bike? You handled the objection by telling him that the bike comes with ABS/advanced safety feature. Since your father was concerned about your safety he might have said okay for a sports bike. Objections come in different formats and there is definitely a solution for each objection .The key to handle objection always comes with your patience and magical smile.

One has to understand that sales process is not always a smooth process, nevertheless it can be made smooth and easy by following few objection handling techniques. Most of the time sales people get disappointed at the time of objection, but one has understand that even objection is a part of sales process. Objection is not the end of sales but it should be treated as the beginning of a good sales process. When you are faced with an objection, don't get annoyed or lose hope instead with a beautiful smile give your best shot. With every sales objection we get to learn about new possibilities and we get to know what are our shortcomings making us prepared for our next sales meeting.

9.1 Price objection

Price is always the first thing a prospect thinks before making a buying decision, price always has remained the biggest objection in the industry. Some prospect is worried about the best price and some prospect look for the lowest price even comprising quality. It really varies from people to people but the ultimate desire of them is always to get the best for what they pay. Many sales person complain and tell that they lost the sales because their competitor had a better price etc...The truth is they lost the sales not because of the competitor but because they failed to explain about the goodies of the product. Many prospects are not worried about the price because they know that they are getting value for money.

Example: "Your prices are very high and at other places price is much cheaper"

Solution: Highlight about the unique selling prepositions of your product which your prospect won't get from your competitor .Make sure you break down your product and services into smaller parts while explaining to them about its value. This will help you overcome the sales objection easily without any hassles.

Give a real life example where a prospect brought a low priced product from your competitor and how they suffered lot of problems. Trigger their lizard brain and it will do the magic by making the prospect buy our product.

9.2 Happy with current product and fear to change objection

All people in this world have a big problem called as comfort zone. Once the prospect get used to a product, they make a comfort zone and fail to explore beyond the product. They have a fear in their mind that if they go beyond the product they will experience danger and uncertainty haunts them. Many people feel they are more than satisfied with the current product and induction of a new product might hamper the current operation or necessity.

Example: "I am more than happy with my current product; I don't need a change now as many things may go wrong."

Solution: Give them facts and figures which are authorized by government bodies or certified agencies, apart from them make them go through a real life example.
Here you can even highlight the profit percentage the people gained by using your product or service. Tell them that a person/company was using the same product and he was happy but after he started using the new product he became delighted. If possible make them talk to the people who are using the current product, or make them meet in person. All this meetings and talking should be only done with prior permission from the concerned people. Also give them a live demonstration of the product or service to feel the "moment of truth" experience.

9.3 Your company is new in the market objection

People always have a feeling that a company from which they are buying should have a good amount of experience in the market. Otherwise they might not take a chance to experiment with your product. This kind of objections is faced by startup companies who are new to the market. Even if the products and services are really good they fail to make an impression because of trust factor. Sometimes this kind of situation becomes a nightmare for the sales person as he finds it hard to sell the product

Example: "How can I trust a company with few months of experience in the market?"

Solution: In this case be honest with them and give them live demonstration of your product. Assure them of good service and get them through case studies where companies benefited from such kind of alliance. Also get them meet or talk with other clients who are already dealing with your company. Try to get testimonials from your clients and present them to your buyers.

Make them understand that competitor's product and your product share the same technology and platform and that they are paying extra for the brand name of their competitor. Don't try to push the prospect too much but instead try to highlight the unique selling preposition of your product. Try to do research on your competitor and make sure to get some customer complaints of your competitor, just present it to your potential buyer. Tell them what can go right by buying your product and what can go wrong if they buy your competitors product.

9.4 Dealing with friends or family connection objection

Clients are always willing to give business to their friend or peers without even checking on their quality or service. It always happens in the industry and becomes a big challenge for sales personals. Sales personals most of the time lose hope and give up following up with the client. This is the best opportunity a sales person can have but the sales person should not lose hope in this situation and should find an opportunity in all situations.

Solution: In this kind of situation we have to make sure that we have patience and do a thorough research on our competitor's product. Make a comparison checklist which shows pros and cons of each product, it should be made with honesty. A person will always buy a product or services which has more competitive advantage. The only thing what we should be careful is that we should never tell bad about our competitors product or services, instead tell them about value addition in our product. After presentation request them to at least give you a chance in the next fiscal year or in the next project.

Example: "I am already dealing with my cousin, who offers me the same products and services"

9.5 Influencer objection

People always say that they need to consult someone important before they make the decision, it might be their manager or their partner or any one whom they trust. This can be sometimes fatal as you have to start the sales conversation from the beginning and definitely the person they introduce might throw up a challenge.

It should not be a sales ending process, rather it should be treated as an opportunity while making the influencer your supporter.

Example: "I need to talk with my general manager on this regard"

Solution: In this scenario make sure that you make a request to include the influencer in the discussion and while in the conversation make sure that you make more conversation with the influencer. While with the influencer make sure that you acknowledge what he is telling and also say like "Mr. Influencer you are in this industry for a long time and you might already know about it". This is a psychological move and it really does work out.

Make sure that you have already done a home work and you are ready with all data sheets and facts, as you are going to face lot of questions. Treat the influencer as the mother of all information's in this world and in this manner instead of opposing you, he will be supporting you.

9.6 I am really busy objection

Sales people always get offended when people say they are busy, it happens most of the time in sales. If the person does not give you a time or date saying when to visit or call next means the sales process is not positive. Sometimes this might be a way to cut you out or to simply say they are least interested in your product.

Example: "I am really busy call or meet me later"

Solution: If the person says he is busy make sure that you ask him/her about the next date and time, when you can get back before you end the conversation. A person who is interested will surely give you a time and date but a person who is least interested will cut the call or end the conversation. By asking them the time and date we can know about their interest level and it equips us with more confidence. If the person says he/she is busy request them for few minutes and if they give us the time, make sure that you only provide with the goodies they will get by dealing with us.

The key to handle this kind of objection is to get a next date/time from the buyer's side. When the next times you call this person make sure that you start the conversation saying "Good morning sir, you had told me to call you on Thursday morning 10: am."

9.7 Procrastination objection

Buyers always ask for more time, this is really dangerous as our competitors get a chance to provide them with better offer. Hence it will be better to close the deal at the earliest.

Delaying the sales process for a long time can make you lose the deal. There may be many other reasons why the particular buyer is delaying the process. Sometimes it might be because of fund shortage or a new project might be starting at a later stage. We have to do a thorough research and find out what is the real reason for the delay and do preparation according to that.

Example: "May be we can discuss after 6 months"

Solution: Explain to the prospect about the offers/discounts your company is providing in this quarter or month, explain to the prospect what he/she will be losing if he is dealing with us after 6 months. Buyer should feel that if he delays that he will be losing out a lot. The key here is to highlight the benefits the buyer is going to get if he is closing the deal within the proposed time.

9.8 Competitors magic objection

When you are having the conversation with the potential buyer and suddenly he tells us that he/she is already dealing with competition product. In this scenario it will be difficult for the sales person to make advancement, but at the same time it gives the sales person a golden opportunity to sow the seeds for future.

Example: "Sorry we are already using another company's product"

Solution: In this scenario you should have done a thorough research before approaching the prospect. More than you know about your product you should know about your competitor's product and this is the key to success. Take a real life example to show how they benefitted from your company's product and what your competitor's product lacked in practicality.

"Sir you are right their cars are very fast ,but sir do you know that it lacks stability and last week only my uncle sold the same model car fearing safety. Now he has brought model R car from our company and he is so much happy, if you want I will make you meet him or talk with him personally"

Offer the buyer a live demo and tell him to feel it for himself, since the prospect might be already using another product request him for an opportunity in the next fiscal or ask him for a reference before ending the sales conversation. Keep doing the follow up and it is very much sure that he/she will give you good business in future.

10. Sales closing techniques

In sales closing is very important, as without it sales will not proceed to the next level. Learning to close effectively and properly might take many months but here in this book you will get the easy way to do it .Closing techniques may vary depending upon different situations and people, as there is no standard operating procedure for sales. Sometimes we just need to use a single closing technique in a particular situation and sometimes we can use multiple closing techniques in a particular situation. The person who has learnt all the effective closing techniques find it very easy to do sales as compared with the person who is still trying to learn from experience. Closing techniques can be more effectively used if it is used after understanding the art of body language. Many sales people get disappointed after they lose sales even after doing good presentation, what they don't understand is that sales only happens if you are equipped with good closing techniques.

Prospect will not buy from you if they don't have strong a conviction about your product and once they have doubts they start raising objections which should be converted to strength of your product. Towards the end of the discussion you should use good closing techniques to close the deals as without it the prospect might delay, cancel or even deal with your competitor. It will be good if you do the closing at the earliest, as giving more time to prospect is not a good move. If you want to understand prospect first we have to understand about our self, as prospect is also a human being. Reasons which make us buy the products are the same reason why prospect buy from us. Closing techniques reassures the prospect on the buying deal and make them to buy only from us at the earliest. If you are not good with your closing techniques then your competitors will surely steal the deal from you.

Closing should be done in such a manner that it creates a ' win win' situation for you as well as for the prospect; they should not feel that you are rushing the prospect to close the deal. This can sometimes create frustration for the prospect and make the situation worse. The timing for the closing can be understood from experience or from the body language signs the prospect is exhibiting during the sales conversation.

Learning closing techniques will give us a competitive advantage over other sales people as we are already prepared to deal with such situations. Never use the closing techniques in the beginning of the sales conversation; rather it should be only used during the end of conversation after tackling objection. Closing techniques not only makes our job easy but also gives prospect more confidence to buy our product. In today's world prospects are very intelligent and we should make sure that we update our knowledge from time to time. Having more knowledge about our product along with competitors product will help in closing the deal. There is no need for you to spend years learning from mistakes; rather it will be better if you master the art of closing.

10.1 5 star close

"Sir our car has the best mileage, resale value, performance, comfort and low maintenance"
5 star close works when the prospect is complaining about high price and undermines about the credibility of our product.

In this scenario sales person can make 5 stars close move in which he presents five important highlights of the product, making a psychological move. It's so powerful move that the prospect gives a positive thought about our product. If

possible have a fact sheet or comparison chart by which we can convince the prospect to close the deal.

10.2 Deliberate Postponement close

"Sir I think it would be better if you take some more time to make the decision, I will give you a call on Monday morning around 10 am to know about your decision"

Deliberate Postponement close works when you have feeling that the prospect might delay the process due to shortage of fund or any other reason, but he/she is almost convinced. Tell them that you understand very well that it's difficult for them to make the decision very soon and it will be better for them to take some more time to think". But make sure that you give a definite time period when you will get back to them; in this manner you make a slot for next appointment.

Before even they tell us that they need time to think, we should give them some time to think about the proposal. It is another powerful psychological move. This make the prospect give a positive thought about the proposal, as they will be appreciating our courtesy.

10.3 Cost versus price with testimonial close

"Sir Price may be high but maintenance cost over the years will compensate the price you are paying today, when you make the comparison with our competitor's vehicle"

This close works when they feel that the price is really high. We have to make them understand about the loss they will be incurring with the purchase of low quality and low price competitor product. We have to show them the report or datasheet in which it clearly mentions the low maintenance cost of our product as compared with competitor's product during a period of time. They will not complain and will be ready to buy from us, once you show them the datasheet or report showing the benefits. You can talk about service cost, replacement cost and spares parts cost etc. We should make them realize that high price of our product is because of good quality materials used and it leads to less maintenance. Also make them talk or meet with a person/company who went for low price of competitor and incurred huge loss. Making prospect meet/talk with your existing prospect for testimonial should be only done with prior permission or else it may be considered as rude.

10.4 Option EFG close

"When do you want your car delivered Monday or Tuesday or Wednesday?"

"Sir would you like to buy red one or blue or yellow?"

This close works when the prospect is lost in thought and has already visited our competitor or has plans to visit.

We cannot give much time for them to think, giving more time to prospect sometimes is not a good move as he can go with our competitor. In order to confuse his mind and restart his mind we can use this close, we can give him three options to choose from. Our tone should be in such a manner that we make an assumption that he /she have already brought the product from us. This move shakes prospects mind and gives us a chance to convince.

10.5 Effort with unique selling preposition close

"Sir our oranges are grown near lush green forest area and we only use toxic free organic fertilizer"

They should feel that we have put lot of effort to produce our product. While explaining we must highlight the value of our product and thus it helps convince prospect easily. Don't ever say your product is good or best but show them value in each part or process of the product. This close should be only used when the prospect feels that the price of the product is very high as compared with our competitor's product. We must politely make them understand the reason why they are paying more for the product. While you are explaining the effort you have put to produce the product, don't forget to highlight the USP of your product. When you explain to prospect about your effort and USP, there is good chance of closing the deal successfully.

10.6 Powerful double manager close

"Sir since you are our premium prospect let me talk to my manager and get you the best deal"

This close can be used with anyone but it will be more effective with the prospect who has already dealt with our company before. Before you use this close you must have informed your manager about it and the offer you are going to give should align with you company policies. Make the prospect feel very special and assure them that you will talk to your managers and try to get the best deal for them. This makes them feel very important and discount or offer provided is highly appreciated.

The catch here is that you are not talking to one manager but two managers in the vertical and when you are doing all this make sure that the prospect is witnessing all this drama. You can first meet your ZM and then after that meet you're SM, when the prospect sees all this he feels that you are taking an extra step for them. If both the managers are not available make sure you call them in front of the prospect. Before you call or meet the managers make sure you already have a pact with them regarding this matter.

10.7 Positive and negative balance sheet

"Sir before you make a decision let us go through the positive and negative of our product lets weigh each one of them"

This close can be only used when prospect has already gone through our competitors benefits but not negatives and is praising competitors product. At this point make sure that you take two sheets of paper and in one sheet of paper draw a line in centre on the left hand side write the positives of your competitor and on the right side write the positives of your company. On the other sheet in the same manner write the negatives of your company in the left side and negatives of competition on the right side. This will make the prospect think about what he is going to lose out and what he is going to gain. This close should only be used if you feel your product has more positives and less negatives. Make sure that you remain honest throughout the process.

10.8 Revisiting and proof close

"I liked your product and definitely will revisit you"

This close has to be used when prospect after presentation is saying that he will get back to you soon. Most of the time there be no get back, henceforth in this scenario tell the prospect that these offers/discount are only available during this particular season. Show them what they will lose out if they don't buy from you now. Before prospect leaves present them with hardcopy showing offers and discounts, in this manner prospect has proof proving our honesty.

10.9 Up to down and down to up in four times close

"Sir you can go for the 3 room flat fully furnished, though expensive but definitely you will like it"

"Sir or you can go for 2 bedroom flat semi furnished, still impressive"

"Sir or else there is 1 bedroom flat, for a very reasonable price and having cupboards."

"Sir there is a flat which is pretty descent for 3 member family but it's not furnished"

Once you find out the budget of prospect, talk about the most expensive product you have in your hand and then carry out four stage operation. Starting from the most expensive to the least expensive, this will definitely make the prospect think that there is no better deal other than this. This can be done in the reverse manner also if the prospect is looking for the most luxurious or most expensive one.

10.10 E - Bluff close

"Sir just gives me a minute let me check in the system for you and see if I can get you any special offer"

This close works when the prospect tells you that he is your regular customer or he will buy from you only if you give him special offer. The moment he/she tells you that, make sure you check your Smartphone, laptop etc. Then randomly take your calculator and do some fast calculations, then finally write it on a piece of paper about the discounts you will offer him. The truth is that you have shown him/her the same offer which is same for all clients, but you have just added little drama to your presentation. Make sure that you don't overdo it, as it can even spoil your reputation in front of the prospect.

10.11 Double butter challenge close

"Sir you might be knowing it already, you are from the same industry"
This close works when the prospect comes with his wife, colleagues or friends to enquire. Always make sure that you try to convince the person who has come with them. Try to talk more with them and also make them feel like they are very knowledgeable person. The reason for this is because once they go out the prospect is going to ask the person who accompanied them. The reason for this is because they trust and value the decision of the person accompanying them. Along with that make sure that you give decent attention to the prospect.

Once the prospect is convinced ask permission whether you can give demo and presentation to other people associated with them.

"Sir since you and wife are now convinced after driving the car, if you want we can give demo to your friends also"

This adds confidence to them and mostly they will say that they are convinced and there is no need for that. This close can be effectively used most of the time and the result of this close is really good.

10.12 Double experience close

"Sir once I give you the demonstration, you can experience it for yourself"
This close works well because you are showing them the demonstration first and then later offering them to experience it for themself. Nothing is more convincing than getting to know about the product before buying.

"Sir let me give the demonstration for the bullet proof vest"

"Sir now you can put the bullet proof vest and experience it for yourself before you make any decision"

10.13 Only for you close

"Sir this offer is only available in metropolitan cities. But since you are our existing customer's friend, we will consider it giving it to you"

This close works when the prospect is your regular prospect or this prospect is a referral case in this case you have to make the prospect feel special. Before you give them the offer make sure that you make them realize why they got the special offer. Also tell them that this offer is special and tell them not to disclose it to any other people. Give them a feeling that we have considered them as a special case because of their loyalty or reference from our loyal customer.

Prospect feels that you are giving him/her special attention with full heart. This makes the prospect buy from you without any hesitation.

10.14 Powerful big shot close

"Sir very recently the same car was brought by famous Actor Mr. X and sir you equally deserve this car assuming your position in society"

This close works when you feel that the prospect has got some ego problems and talks negative about your product. We find it difficult to convince this kind of prospect with our presentation.

In this scenario tell the prospect about a celebrity or a big shot in the market that had recently brought the product from your company.

Make the prospect feel that he also deserves the product as he is equally prominent in society. This manner you are comparing prospect with the big shot in the society or market.

This makes the prospect stop talking negative about your product and also prospect thinks that this product has got brand value. This is the same reason why celebrities are made brand ambassador.

10.15 Bonus writes down close

"Sir would you mind to write down the important things you are looking out in our product"

Writing is more powerful than speaking; first make them to write down the important things they are expecting from our product. Once they write it down, write down the advantages of your product near their writing. In this manner you show the prospect that your product is a good choice for them, as it carries more benefits than prospects expectation. This close works when you feel that prospect is more into rational thinking. If possible also present the prospect with awards or recognition which your product has bagged over the years with some statistical data.

10.16 Stereotype breaker close

"Sir you don't need to buy the product at all this is just part of our marketing"

Prospect always will be very much defensive even before we are going to talk with them because of their stereotype thinking.

Prospects always thinks that we are sales people and we only will talk good about our product as we are selling it, hence they tend to form a defensive barrier. They break this barrier only when we tell them that we are doing it for the purpose of marketing and they don't need to buy from us. In this manner psychologically we make them listen to us and they accept our product without many hassles.

11. Referrals

Referrals are very much important in sales, as it gives good prospect oriented leads rather than cold leads. The chances of closing the prospect leads are better than the cold leads, in case of prospect leads there are chance of 55% and in case of cold leads there are chances of 23-29%.In a recent study it was noticed that only few sales people attempt to ask for referrals and only depended on direct sales leads.

The best way to have successful sales in all season is to have referral case. You should make sure that you ask referral from each prospect or customer, as you have nothing to lose. Whether you get sales or not, asking referral should be your priority at the end of sales process.

"Sir I hope that you are really satisfied with our services and products. If you give us some referral case, it will be really helpful"

"Sir I know that you are currently using our competitors product, henceforth I wish you all the best. I will be really happy if you can at least give us some referrals"

There are many sales people who just survive in referral cases; referral case never lets your sales pipeline dry out. The chances of getting reference will be more, if you ask the customer after the delivery of products or services. A satisfied prospect or customer will definitely give you more positive prospect lead.

Make sure that you make the prospect or customer talk to reference before you approach the referral case. This will make your job easy and convincing the prospect will be piece of cake. In case if the prospect or customer hesitate to talk to the referral case on your behalf, make sure that you collect as much information as possible from the prospect or customer before talking to the referral case. While you make call to the referral case for taking appointment make sure that you inform them how you got their details. Make sure that you always keep the prospect or customer in loop with the referral case as this will again help you with more referrals and respect. Sales people most of the time forget to keep the prospect or customer in loop after they get referral. This should never be exercised, as it makes them have a feeling that we lack gratitude.

"Sir I contacted reference Mr. X, he told me that I can meet him on 23rd morning. I am really thankful that you gave me a good referral."

4 tips to get good referrals

1. Ask referral after delivery and not closing
2. Provide the prospect or customers with a small gift/rewarding system for the referral.
3. Give prospect or customer good service and make sure prospect or customer is very happy
4. Reward the prospect or customer providing referral

When you meet the reference case make sure that you tell the referral case how close you are to the prospect or customer and why they brought the product from you. In this manner you convince the referral case that your product has got good credibility and brand value in the market. In case of a referral case, the amount of objections will be limited and closing will be very much easy.

Before approaching the referral case make sure that you do a thorough research and get as much information as possible from the prospect. You may even get reference case from your friends, peers, family or even colleagues, but make sure that you don't miss out any. A prospect or customer will give a good reference only when the prospect or customer feels that referral case will benefit from the same product which the prospect or customer is using. It has also been noted in the industry that a sales person giving good sales and services to customers receives many referrals even without asking for it.

<u>Advantages of referral</u>

1. You can bypass gatekeeper
2. Your leads are already qualified
3. Your competition becomes minimal
4. You get more sales even in off season

12. Follow up

Sales follow up is very important and can do miracles. People think that just by doing good presentation and executing good closing techniques one can achieve sales. There are two types of follow up, one is done before sales to get sales and one is done after sales to get referrals. Even today many experienced sales people forget to do the follow up and only rely on sure cases. Follow up can change enquiry to leads and leads to prospect thus saving time and resources. Sales people should not have a misconception that by just meeting many people they can get more sales; it can be only true if they do appropriate follow up. Many of the time we hear sales people saying that they are doing hard work and yet not getting good results. The reason for this is that they are meeting many people but fail to do the follow up. They assume that the prospect will call them for sales, we have to understand that it is not the prospects requirement rather our requirement to sell the product. Prospect has got many ways through which he can buy the product, so it becomes our requirement to do the follow up.

Status of leads

1. Cold
2. Warm
3. Hot

Sales people should make sure that they record the details of the people or leads they are meeting. It should be done either by using a software or a excel sheet. But make sure that you record the status of the leads. A cold lead is one in which the prospect don't wants to buy the product, warm lead is the one in which prospect might buy the product and Hot one is the one in which the prospect is sure to buy the product.

The biggest beauty of follow up is that it helps you to convert cold leads to warm lead and then warm lead to hot lead, which is also called as a hot prospect. During the sales follow up make sure that you keep the conversation short and informative with courtesy.

Sample follow up sheet

SNO	NAME	DESIGNATION	COMPANY	MOBILE	EMAIL	ADDRESS	NEXT FOLLOW UP	STATUS	REMARKS
1	RAVI	PURCHASE EXE	TYU INC	8967869645	INC@INC.COM	RITU COMPLEX	THURSDAY 10 AM	COLD	NIL
2	HAMSA	CEO	KOP LTD	6768945765	KOP@KOP.COM	DEV AVENUE	FRIDAY 4 PM	WARM	NIL
3	SEETHA	FOUNDER	MK INTERNATIONAL	9875689678	MK@ETP.IN	HARITHA COMPLEX	22-Oct	HOT	NIL

Always make sure that you give different colours to the lead status and keep updating the next follow up status. So that every day morning when you look at the sheet you know whom to call or meet. In this manner you will not miss out any meetings or schedules. Many companies even provide their sales executives with iPod and laptops in which they maintain the prospect details and it also has the facility to inform the executives about the next follow up date. Maintaining in excel sheet can only be feasible if the data is very small, but if you are maintaining too much data then you have to go with some software which will compliment your purpose. After meeting the prospect make sure that you send a thanks giving email enclosing all the details of your company, but make sure that it is not too bulky or colourful. Before leaving from the premises of the prospect or at the end of cold call make sure that you ask the prospect when you should meet or call them next. We should make sure that we get the exact time and date, also be sure to make a note of it in our software or excel sheet.

"Sir since you are busy now, when should I call you next? Can you please tell me the date and time, so that I don't disturb you during your busy hours?"

"Sir when should I call you next"

"Mr. John when should we keep our next meeting"

Most of the sales people complain saying that follow up is a very difficult and prospect sometimes hang up. This is because we fail to get the time and date from the prospect and we call them randomly. This really disturbs them and hence we lose our chance to close the deal. When you make the next call or visit make sure that you mention that you have called the prospect as per schedule.

"Good morning sir my name is Rakish from dye company, you had told me to call you today at 10 am"

Always make sure that you do this procedure during every follow up so that you convert cold lead to hot lead or hot prospect. You can text him through social media like WhatsApp or face book, only if you are in good rapport with the prospect and he has shared you his personal number. During the time between first meeting and sales closing, always makes sure to wish the prospect on special occasions or festivals. This is another way by which we can keep in touch with the prospect and prospect keeps us in mind thus not giving chance for our competitors product. Never invade their privacy by messaging them during odd hours of the day or stalking them. They should feel that we are professionals and we respect their personal space or time.

"SHI group of companies wish you and your family happy diwali"

Don't lose hope, if the prospect says that they need more than 5 months to make the decision. In our excel sheet or software write it down as warm lead, as the prospect is willing to buy from us but because of some other reasons he needs time. Maybe Competitor's contract might be expiring in 5 months of time. There is no other fun job like sales, it becomes a real game in which our job is to convert cold leads to hot leads and this happens with follow up. If you are dealing with a cold lead make sure that you don't push them too much for sales, as pushing will only spoil sales. Don't lose hope in dealing with rejection and cold leads as they make most part of the sales. In this scenario make sure to pay a personal visit to the prospect, but make sure that you don't talk about your product or business. In this manner you are telling the prospect that more than selling the product, you respect them and you are very much courteous. In this manner you can build good relationship with the customers and prospects. They might buy from you in the future or even give you part of their requirement. There are even cases when cold leads have even given good referral to the sales people due to follow up. We can avoid annoying the customer, if we can ask them the preferred medium of contact.

"Sir good morning please be assured, I did not come here to sell. I was just passing by and I thought of wishing you happy diwali personally"

Medium for follow up

1. Telesales
2. Social media
3. Personal visit
4. Email etc

Some sales people find it difficult to meet up with VIP prospects, in this scenario best way to do sales follow up will be through email. Write up an email which is not too lengthy or colorful reminding the prospect of the next meeting or procedure. Next type of follow up is done after the sales and is as important as before sales follow up.

Many sales people think that the sales process has ended with the delivery of the product, but in reality it has just begun. Sales people always complain of not getting enough referrals after sales, it is because they have not done enough after sales follow up.

Customers always feel that sales people are mean people and they only are courteous and caring till they get sales from them. We have to break this kind of stereo type thinking by even doing follow up after sales.

After sales follow up process

Follow up after 3 days –Ask about the feedback and address their grievance

Follow up after 15 days-Make a personal visit and reassure about the quality of product

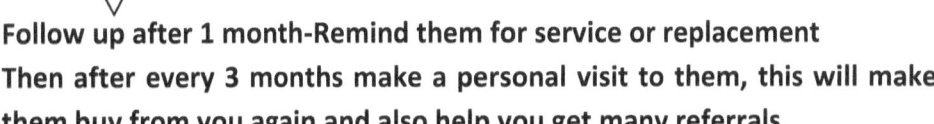

Follow up after 1 month-Remind them for service or replacement

Then after every 3 months make a personal visit to them, this will make them buy from you again and also help you get many referrals.

After sales follow up gets you more referrals and this become one of your sales pipelines. In this manner you are creating more and happier satisfied customer willing to give you more referrals.

Advantages of follow up

1. Get referrals
2. Happy customer
3. Get feedback to improvise
4. Continuous improvement
5. Analyze results

13. Sales public speaking and presentation

If you ask someone what is their biggest fear they will definitely say public speaking, people fear to do public speaking more than they fear to die. One of the biggest nightmare of a sales person is to present himself in front of an audience and do the sales presentation. As sales personal you might need to do many presentations throughout your sales career. Good presentation is always rewarded with lot of enquiries, leads or even hot prospects. Sales presentation may be done in front of few decision makers or even in front of a large audience. As sales people we should not say that it is the job of marketing department, rather you should take it as your initiative and utilize every chance you get to do the presentation. In this book we will discuss how we can conquer our fears while doing the presentation and how we can make it more effective. Sales presentation can be done at the prospects premises or even it can be carried out in our company conference room. Always make sure that you are well prepared before the presentation even giving importance to minute details.

Preparation before sales presentation

1. **Product knowledge:** There is no other thing like product knowledge which gives you so much confidence. Your audience will surely assume that you are a product genius and will definitely ask you as many questions as possible. You have to know about your product as well as your competitor's product so that you can make good comparison and highlight the USP of your product.

2. Dressing and grooming: You should make sure that you look in your best form during the presentation. Wear your best tie and suit for the presentation, overall you should become the centre of attraction .People should feel that this is the best way in which one can dress and present oneself. In this manner we can make sure that we make our first impression in front of the crowd.

3. Technical equipments: Many times during the presentation it happens that the projector goes blank or there is loose connection in the wiring. Even sometimes it is noticed that the speaker does not know how to use the slide changer or the newly installed projector. One must make sure that before they enter for presentation, whether in their company conference room or outside hall they should have pre checked all the equipments .This practice is done to avoid embarrassment in front of the audience and boost your confidence.

4. Desktop cleaning: When you make the presentation using your laptop at some point of time you might accidently show up your desktop and it becomes your duty to make it free from your personal photos or unwanted files. Make sure that your desktop has a standard background and this will again boost professionalism. In industry quite often sales people gets into the embarrassing situation, when they accidently show up their desktop with their personal pictures.

5. Researching: It will be really helpful if we know about our audience. We have to know about their age, designation, company details; location etc.It gives you more confidence and also earns you the wits to answer their questions smartly. This helps you to make them understand how your product can cater to their needs or demands. You can also do a thorough research on the products they are currently using, this way we can give those facts and figures leading to more convincing answers.
"Ms Sarah you are form XYZ village ,you might be knowing how difficult it is to get clean drinking water and our water filter surely addresses that."

6.Presentation program: There are many presentation program available in the market and Microsoft PowerPoint programs remains to be the most simple and powerful tool .While making your presentation slides make sure that your presentation slide follows few important points.

1. Use simple but attractive design
2. Don't use too dark colours for presentation
3. Use bullet points to highlight points
4. Usage of text and pictures
5. Use only small videos 5-10 minutes maximum
6. Avoid paragraph or cluttered format
7. Usage of san serif font
8. Use a story to start the presentation
9. Facts and figures shown should be in simple form

Don'ts during presentation

1. Never walk in front of the projector light
2. Don't show your back while standing in the stage
3. Don't use your fingers to highlight points, instead use laser pointer
4. Don't use vulgar words or adult jokes
5. Don't show aggression towards audience
6. Don't chew or eat during presentation
7. Don't avoid eye contact with audience
8. Don't include religious or political talks in presentation
9. Don't bluff if you don't know about the topic
10. Don't do the presentation without smiling.

Techniques for eradicating stage fear

1. Who is intelligent? Technique: Sometimes the audience will be new to you and all the new faces might cause nerve tremors for you. In this techniques ask a difficult question to the audience related to the presentation topic and see who answers it. In this manner you gain confidence and get a chance to look at everyone thus understanding the pitch of your audience. If someone answers correctly, appreciate them and then relate this with your presentation topic and carry on with your presentation. This technique is used when the audience size is more than 10. This technique is very much effective and gives the speaker courage to carry on with the presentation.

2.Wave scanning technique: This technique is also used to check the unknown audience .While you are making a presentation make sure that you start scanning faces of people from the left side of the hall to the right side of the hall and then to the back end of right side to the back end of left side. Eye contact should not be for more than 2 seconds and this way you give a felling to the audience that you are looking at everyone all the time. This gives you good confidence and this also makes you not end up looking at someone who makes you nervous. This technique should be only used when the audience size is more than 50.

3. Breaking the session hacker: Session hackers are the people who give nightmares to sales people. They are often people with either more knowledge or no knowledge and sometimes might even ask you some stupid questions. Make sure that you do not humiliate this kind of people, but answer them politely .Sessions hackers can sometimes spoil the whole decorum of the sales presentation. If you don't know the answer for hacker's question, make sure that you acknowledge the hackers interest to know about the particular topic. After that tell him that you are about to present about this in the coming slide and it will be better for you to discuss it during that time. In between that try to find about it from your seniors or others sources to clear hackers doubt. Some hackers may deliberately try to spoil the decorum by asking you unrelated questions again and again. These kinds of hackers are attention seekers and want too much appreciation. In this case make sure that ask them some easy questions and when they answer, make sure that you appreciate them in front of the whole crowd.

After a while make them to explain about few topics and when they try to do, add some points to it and appreciate the hacker. In this way you tell the audience and hacker that you are the smart one. There is another way through which you can deal with hacker, in this technique you make the hacker answer the question asked by another member from the audience. Hacker will lose his credibility, if he is unable to answer questions asked by other audience member. In this manner you can take control of the dominant hackers in all situations.

4. Social technique: It will be really good if you make the audience give an introduction about them before the presentation. This helps you to understand about them and plan your script. In between the presentation make the audience share their view points and experience on other products or competition. This again gives you more confidence and the whole presentation becomes like a social gathering with your friends.
Note: Day before your sales presentation makes sure that you have good night sleep and you drink plenty of water making you look fresh.

14. Motivtional quotes

In life always have a plan B as you can't confirm plan A will work.....but if plan B also fails formulate plan C.....in short never ever give up no matter how many times you have to fail.....as your happiness lies in fulfilling your dreams

MITHUN DEVADAS

Latest strategy for success is innovation....innovation and innovation....

MITHUN DEVADAS

If your soul is sweet and light means it will float like helium balloon ....but if your soul is filled with ego... selfishness...etc...It might float but not for very long

MITHUN DEVADAS

Engaging your brain to be busy with lot of work during high times of demotivation and negativity turns the negative energy into positive energy.

MITHUN DEVADAS

People will put you down...ignore you....make fun of you and even harass you....People might also demotivate you......You will only get hurt ... if you absorb negative energy ...If you ignore all this and stay positive life will be happy....Don't ever take things into heart as nothing is permanent in life.....even your worries and problems.

MITHUN DEVADAS

It is leadership that you should aim for and not manager role, managers always fail in the long run but leaders never do. Becoming a leader is not easy but once you become a leader you transform yourself and people around you as next level leaders

MITHUN DEVADAS

Mix innovation with creativity in whatever you do.....trust me it will trigger the chain reaction leading to "Success".

MITHUN DEVADAS

Thank god that he is giving us problems, actually problems are like training manuals which make us fit and sturdy for more difficult times ahead.

MITHUN DEVADAS

108

Words without action is like gun without bullet.

MITHUN DEVADAS

Like you breath try to think, like you eat try to innovate, like you blink try to work, like you sleep try to relax and one day you will be at the top of this world.

MITHUN DEVADAS

In life sometimes we meet people who become a history....some become mystery and some become the reason for our success.......honour them.

MITHUN DEVADAS

We don't have time to learn from our mistakes in this highly competitive world. Better learn from others mistakes, who are successful now. Learning becomes fruitful when we execute our understanding.

MITHUN DEVADAS

Success is a mock tail of Hard work, smart work, innovation, dedication etc.....served in a glass of consistency.

MITHUN DEVADAS

In life trust only two things, your intuition and experience................they are never wrong.
MITHUN DEVADAS

Wisdom begins when you understand that you are not the most powerful person in this world, you are not the most beautiful person in this world...........................you are not the most intelligent person in the world..................But when you feel you are just an invisible part of the infinite mighty universe.

MITHUN DEVADAS

Don't wait for things to happen in our journey of life, for auspicious things to happen in life............have an attacker's mentality.........a go get it attitude.............a positive attitude.

MITHUN DEVADAS

Experience is not about the years you are spending, but experience is the understanding of small things as you go.

MITHUN DEVADAS

If there is a uphill then there is a downhill, if there is night there is a day..............if there is upstream there is a downstream.................same way when you are down and feel that you have lost everything in life, just wait for the right time...................in short have patience and see the magic.

MITHUN DEVADAS

Leadership is a precious affair; it is not just a word.

MITHUN DEVADAS

Always thank your enemies as they are our true friends, as they show our mistakes and always keep a watch on us. Thus giving us a chance to improve ....giving us perfection and competitive edge

MITHUN DEVADAS

Empathy is the soul of sales

MITHUN DEVADAS

If we stop breathing we will die and if we start giving up in life we will not succeed, so keep breathing and face life with a smile.....a never ending smile.

MITHUN DEVADAS

www.ingramcontent.com/pod-product-compliance
Lightning Source LLC
Chambersburg PA
CBHW020923180526
45163CB00007B/2858